Body Bones

Shelley Rotner
and David A. White

Holiday House / New York

To my dear friend Alison—S. R.
To Doug Norman, for teaching me
how to observe and see the world—D. A. W.

The publisher would like to thank pediatrician Dr. Kristin D'Aco
for checking the art and text of this book for accuracy.

Text copyright © 2014 by Shelley Rotner and David A. White
Photographs copyright © 2014 by Shelley Rotner
Illustrations copyright © 2014 by David A. White
All Rights Reserved
HOLIDAY HOUSE is registered in the U.S. Patent and Trademark Office.
Printed and Bound in March 2014 at Toppan Leefung, DongGuan City, China.
www.holidayhouse.com
First Edition
1 3 5 7 9 10 8 6 4 2

Library of Congress Cataloging-in-Publication Data
Rotner, Shelley, author, photographer.
Body bones / Shelley Rotner and David A. White. — First edition.
pages cm
Audience: Ages 6-10.
Audience: Grades 4 to 6.
ISBN 978-0-8234-3162-5 (hardcover)
1. Bones—Juvenile literature. 2. Skeleton—Juvenile literature.
3. Anatomy, Comparative—Juvenile literature.
I. White, David A. (David Alan), 1973- illustrator, author. II. Title.
QM101.R68 2014
573.76—dc23
2013044989

We all have a skeleton made of many bones.
Bones are alive. They grow as you grow.
As your bones grow longer, you grow taller.

Bones have special jobs to do. They give you your shape.
They support, protect, and help you move.

Your bones fit together like a puzzle to form your skeleton. Just like the framework of a house, your body has a framework of bones.

You would not be able to stand up without your skeleton.

The bones on the top of your head are called a skull.
Your skull protects your brain just like a bicycle helmet.

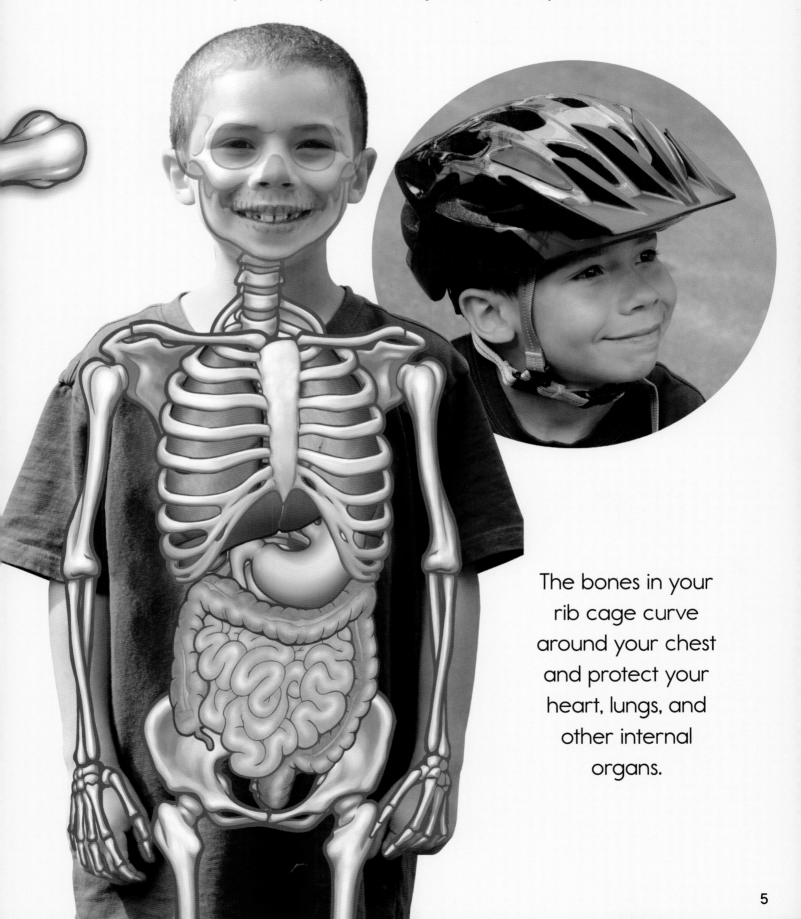

The bones in your
rib cage curve
around your chest
and protect your
heart, lungs, and
other internal
organs.

Many other animals have bones too. Animal skeletons each have different shapes with a different number of bones that help creatures walk, run, swim, fly, or move.

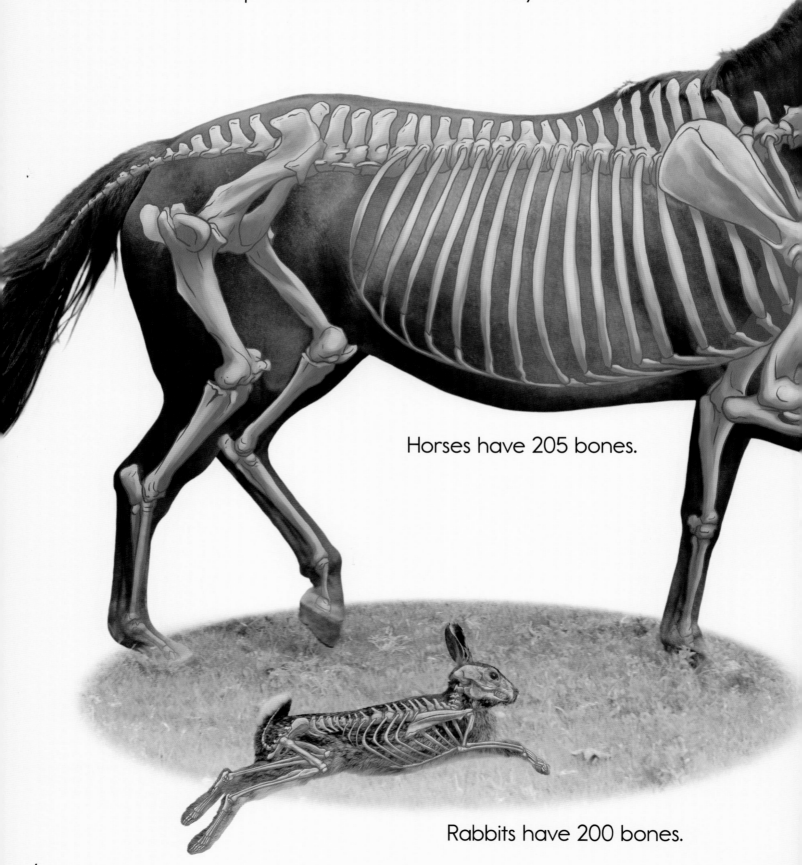

Horses have 205 bones.

Rabbits have 200 bones.

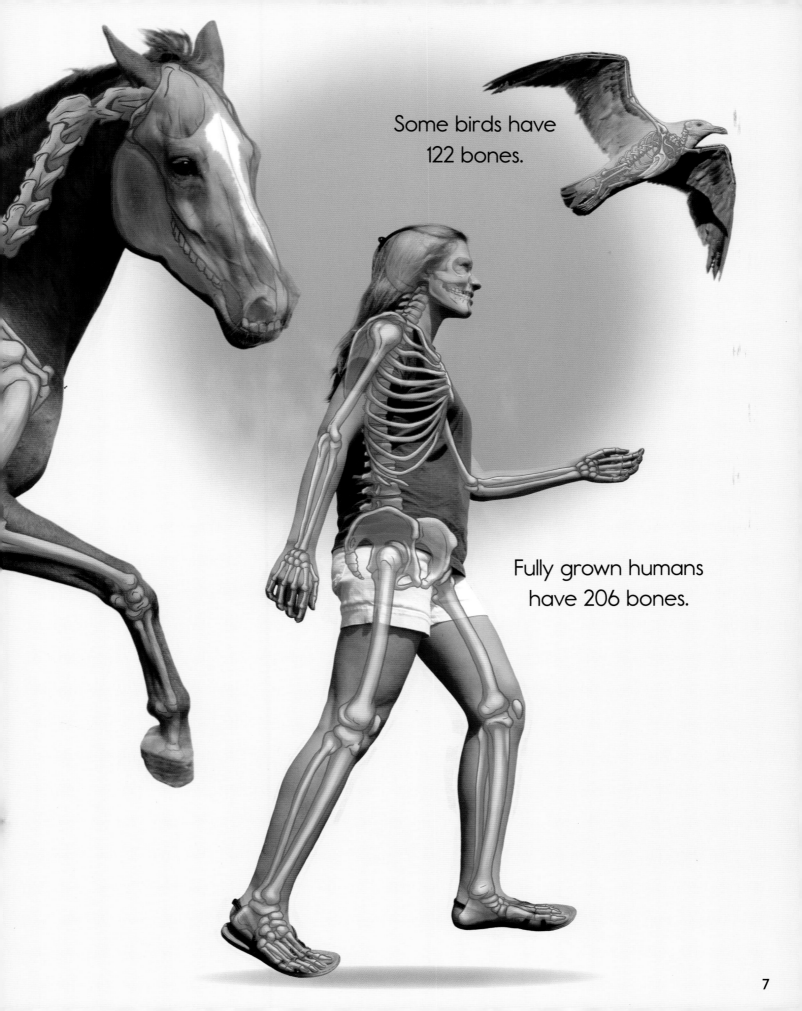

Some birds have 122 bones.

Fully grown humans have 206 bones.

Snakes have anywhere from 600 to 1,200 bones.
Because they can have as many as 400 bones in their spine,
snakes are extremely flexible.

Fish have hundreds of bones. Their skeletons are shaped like arrows. This shape allows them to move easily through water. Larger fish can have as many as 1,500 bones.

When you're born, your bones are soft. They get harder as you grow. They keep growing until you are about twenty-five years old.

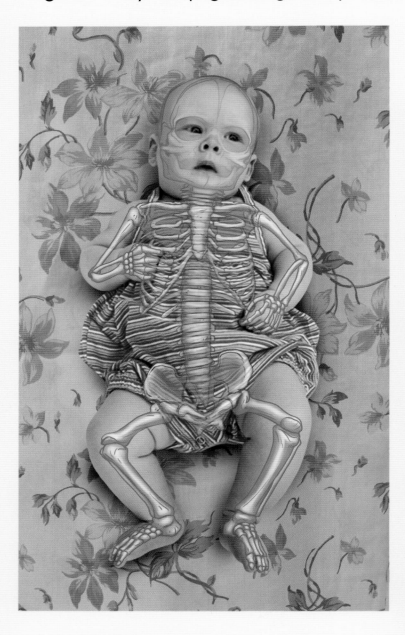

Babies are born with 270 bones and then some of them fuse, or grow together, until they have 206 bones in all.

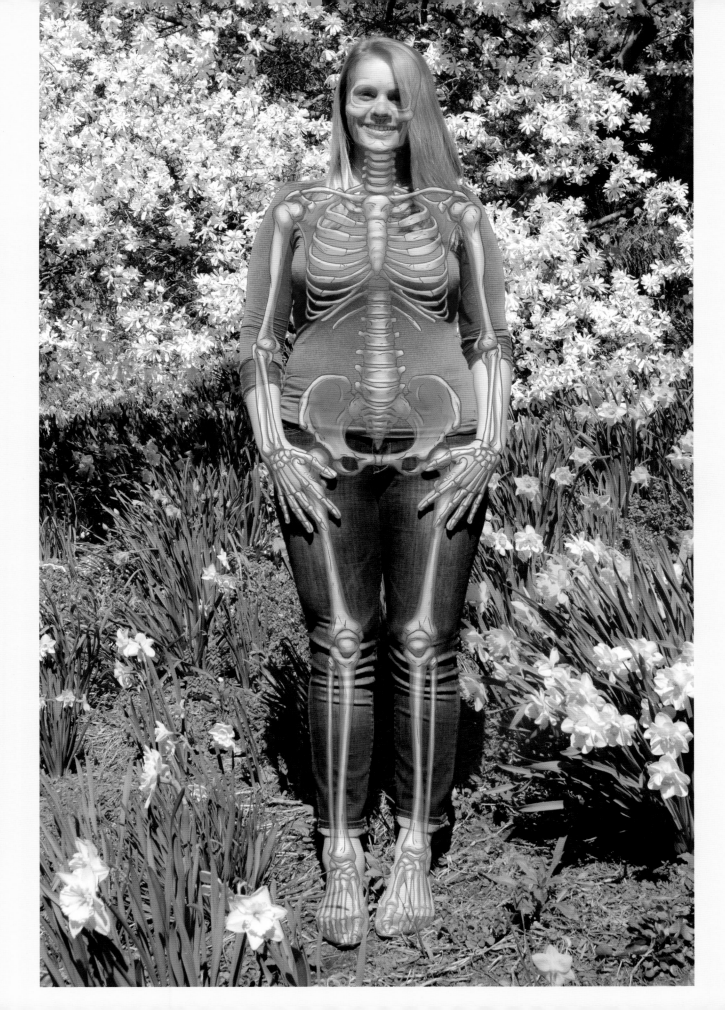

Tadpoles are baby frogs.
At first they only have
soft cartilage. As they grow
older and change into frogs,
the cartilage turns into bones.

Skeletons are usually symmetrical, or the same on both sides.

Turtles are born with rib cages that fuse together
with the spine and pelvis to form a shell.

Elephants have long, thick leg bones that help support their big size and weight.

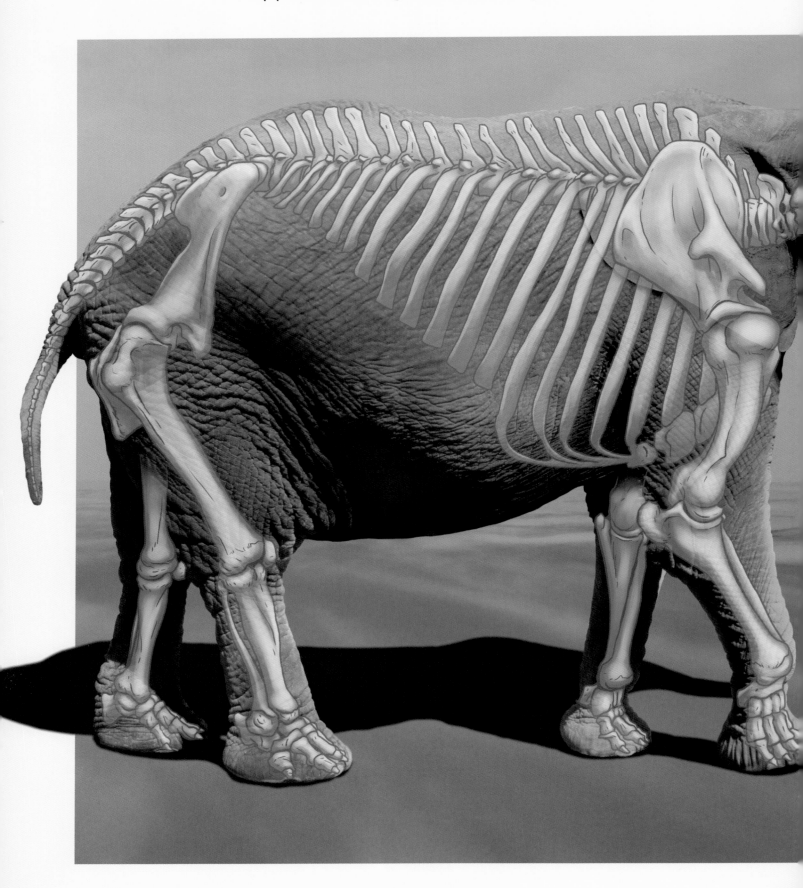

Birds have light, hollow
bones and large wing
bones for flying.

Bones are hard and come in all shapes and sizes. There
are long bones, curved bones, and even flat bones.

Teeth are bones too! Teeth are covered with enamel and are the hardest part of your body. Different kinds of teeth are good at doing different things.

Cows have flat teeth for chewing plants.

Cats have pointy teeth for biting.

Birds don't have any teeth, but they have
beaks that work somewhat like teeth.

Beavers have wide, chisel-shaped teeth
for cutting through wood.

Human children have 20 teeth
by the time they are three years old.

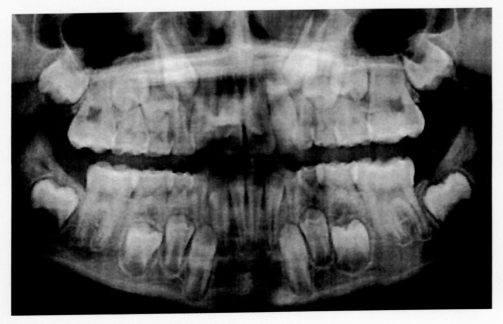

Eventually their
baby teeth fall out,
and 32 permanent,
or adult, teeth
replace them.

Crocodiles have 64 to 69 teeth.
Every time a tooth falls out
a new one grows in its place.

Puppies have 28 teeth. Just like humans, dogs lose their baby teeth.
A full-grown dog has 42 permanent teeth.

Not all animals have bones. Jellyfish are soft
and don't have any bones at all.

Sharks have skeletons made of flexible cartilage instead
of bone, but they have hundreds of bone teeth.
Whenever a tooth falls out, a new one replaces it.

Insects and crustaceans don't have any bones inside their bodies. Instead, they have hard exoskeletons that cover the outside of their bodies.

Bones are made up of different layers.
They're hard on the outside and soft on the inside.

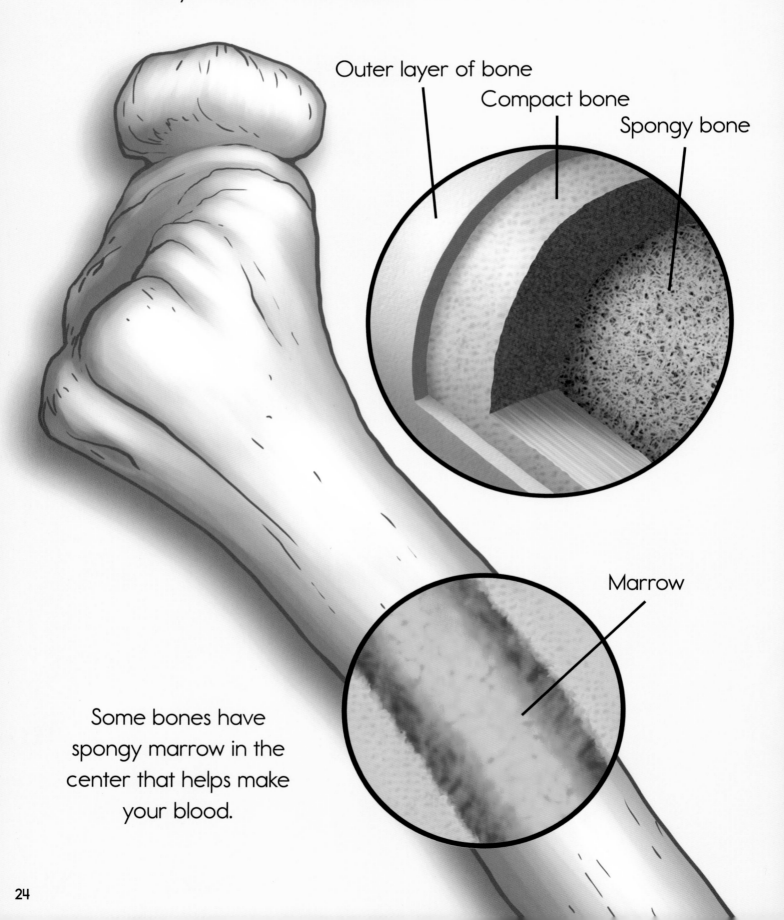

Outer layer of bone

Compact bone

Spongy bone

Marrow

Some bones have spongy marrow in the center that helps make your blood.

Some horns are made of bone.

When bones are buried in the ground for a long time and the conditions are just right, they can turn into fossils. That's how we learn about dinosaurs and other animals from long ago.

Your bones are held together by strong, stretchy tendons and ligaments that are like rubber bands. Muscles push and pull your bones and help your body move.

Your elbows and knees are connected by joints. There are several joints in each finger. Joints let your bones bend and twist so you can run and play.

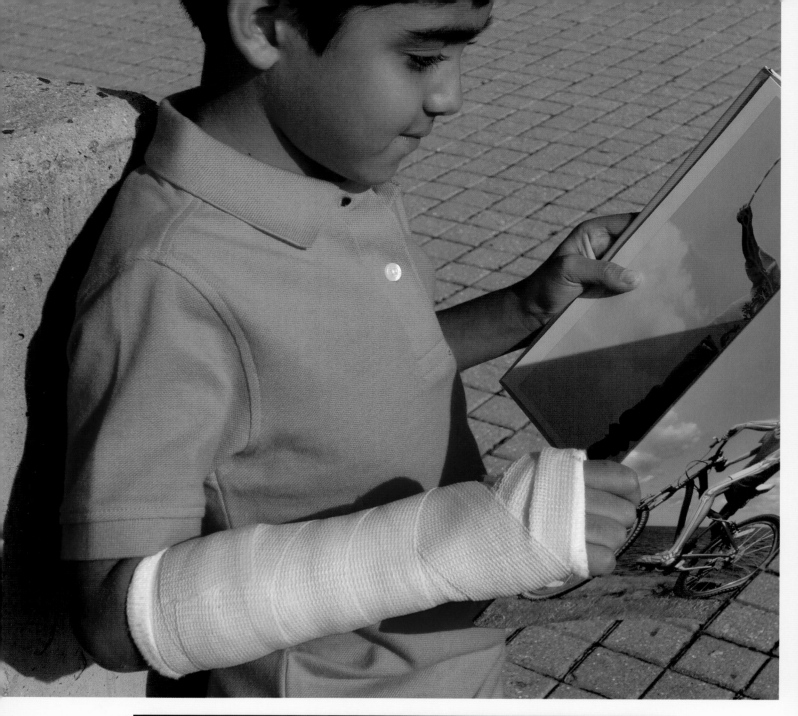

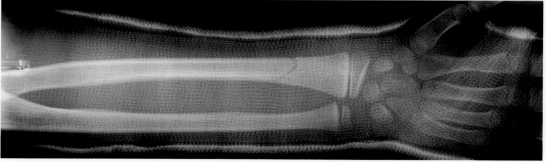

Bones are strong and flexible, but they can break. The body starts to repair broken bones right away.